tinder tactics

by
Hayley O'Hare

Designed by Crazy Monkey Creative
Photographs from Shutterstock
© 2016 Scarlet Editions/Hayley O'Hare

Printed in China

Scarlet
Editions

'Tinder' has recently replaced 'Smith'
as the most common last name
on people's phones.

contents

the world of tinder

Welcome to the world of tinder.

This is your comprehensive guide to tinder success. Inside this book you are going to find some real life examples on what goes down, how to react, some helpful (and maybe not so helpful) tips and suggestions on how to take on this fickle world and become your country's reigning tinder champion.

As this book has landed in your lap, it suggests to me that you are either seriously considering getting involved in the app or you're on your 3rd profile and need serious guidance. Either way congratulations!

Sit back, relax and make sure that your phone is fully charged.

tinder

(tin-der)

noun

1) a highly flammable material or preparation formerly used for catching the spark from a flint and steel struck together for fire or light

2) any dry substance that readily takes fire from a spark

3) a dating app for the masses

Never to be confused with...

grindr

noun

This fatal mistake could be both highly embarrassing and leave one feeling very uncomfortable!

signing up

Signing up is a piece of piss, as long as you've got a smart phone of some description (it is the 21st century!).

Download the app.

If you're a facebooker, tinder does all the leg work for you, selecting three of your finest profile pics, uses your first name and kindly sharing your age (fear not, Facebook will not announce to your friends list that you are on tinder - it's completely anonymous!). If you are not Facebook friendly then you will have to manually upload your selected shots, type in your name, age and occupation all by yourself - exhausting I know.

this takes minutes!!!

Tinder will then ask permission to 'use your location' by accessing your mobile GPS (yawn), to which you agree. You can dictate how far you're willing to travel using the 'maximum distance' slider found in the discovery settings alongside 'gender' (get this right - don't be greedy) and desired 'age range'.

Now you are pretty much up and ready to rumble.

let the cream see the cracker!

profile

Let's get started.

You're going to need the perfect profile - now I never said this was going to be easy...
Remember first impressions count, this could potentially change the rest of your life... no pressure.

Think personal sales pitch. This is your opportunity to lure someone in. Keep your profile short and sweet. It should contain a handful of pics and perhaps a brief bio about yourself... do be modest, don't ramble, remember less is more.

Upload a knockout front profile pic, now this needs to be a recent snap, and ideally a realistic resemblance of you. Avoid the 'bedroom mirror selfie' but if you can't resist, do make your bed and pick up your dirty washing!

Your main pic should be all about you!
SMILE, feel free to have a pic with some friends and try to look friendly. If you have children maybe slip in a little cute shot as a subtle hint but don't go on about it.

A perfect profile should be intriguing, leave the viewer wanting more and result in endless matches.

Get ready to rake in those dates!

15

left or right swipe?

So your banging profile is up and
running and we are good to go!!
Now it's time to start sifting through the
pile of fellow tinder users (which always
reminds me of a deck of cards?!).
I recommend a quick scan over the
pics and bio, if they don't make
you want to vomit then swipe
right - think 'quick fire round'.

There's no point obsessing over
people's profiles showcasing their finest
filtered selfies and holiday snaps, you
need to communicate with
these beings...

Do not be too precious.

You will be surprised how many people
you match with and also how many
people are not up for a chat... don't
be put off by this, keep going.

Let's be honest, most people are looking for their future long-term partner or somebody to procreate with and you aren't going to find them sitting indoors staring at your phone.

I'm not saying be desperate. REMEMBER - this is anonymous, people won't know you've liked them unless they like you, which then equals a match, so hey presto!!!!

Spot someone you know?
Give them a right swipe ;)
They've probably done the same...

Have no shame!

19

messaging

Like someone and they like you back?
You have yourself a match my
tinder lover!

You are now cordially invited to the
world of messaging.

This is tough territory and there are
no set rules to getting this right.

So who makes the first move?
Some go all traditional and think
the man should make the first
move, whilst some simply swoop
in with a one-liner or often just an
original 'hey'.

Sadly a small minority think that it's OK to send nude photos.

WTF?

Block any that send you nudes and carry on sifting through your matches/stock.

As a tinder expert and seasoned pro, sadly I don't have the answers here.

My best advice? Get yourself a drink and a mate at your side to help. If your bff is busy then send them endless annoying screenshots in desperation whilst asking for their opinion.

bad profiles

The anonymous profile
Playing hide and seek? A bit shy? Don't want their work colleagues to spot they're a tinder user?
Nope afraid not, you can bet your bottom dollar these buggers have a spouse, offspring coming out of their ears and have got a driving ban, amongst some other offences.

NEXT

The couple account
'attractive, athletic couple looking for like-minded to be adventurous with'

Now this is slightly more unusual but not unheard of, so don't be caught out...
These folk are not looking for someone to climb Kilimanjaro with or a buddy for a sailing holiday... They may be after a little bit more.

You have been warned.

The badly doctored profile pic

As fabulous as you may think you appear photographed looking bronzed in Gran Canaria, DO NOT be tempted to cut your ex out of a photo. People will spot any foul play a mile off and you will look like an absolute plonker.

If you do match with someone who appears to have cut out an old flame, ignore their messages, shame on them for being too lazy to get a mate to take a new pic and upload it.

DRUM ROLL please for my particular favourite .....

The wedding pic profile

Seems hard to believe I know, but these corkers are out there floating about in all their glory (fantastic screenshot material).

Perhaps they're in an open relationship? More than likely they don't know how to use the tinder app or the shiny new iphone they got for Christmas. If this is the case, they deserve to be hit round the head with it and sent back to school.

left swipe!!

x

dating

Bingo you have a date... hurrah!

Make an effort, do your hair, don't eat a truck load of garlic the night before, carry some peppermints with your rape alarm.

Arrive on time - be punctual, not early. There's nothing fashionable about being late...
It's just bloody rude.

DO NOT overdress!!!!!!!

Use the power of Google to assess the arranged meeting place and pick appropriate attire. Plan ahead if need be.

Be nice, smile, avoid Indian food and don't order the spag bol.

When meeting a date always let at least one person know where you are headed and approximate meeting times.

Share your location with all your whatsapp homies but be prepared for them to appear at a window and spy.

A few different options for when it's not going well...

You could fake an illness?

Carry a taser? (technically illegal... don't).

Let off a smoke flare? (we didn't check if this was illegal but it most probably is when you're outside a marine environment).

If you feel uneasy, form a plan to get away. Above all else, stay safe and make sure friends and family are aware of your movements.

alcohol

Too many people (and this certainly includes me!) believe alcohol consumption is important and can ensure conversation is free-flowing and a little less awkward.

Try not to get too lubricated before an initial meeting as this can be frowned upon. A half-cut date can prove quite a distraction to the other party.

If a date is going well, drink can flow freely - in this scenario just try to remain dignified!

It's my personal preference to avoid shots of any kind and of course any drink that's blue in colour.

If the date is boring but you happen to know it's their treat this time, then why not just get pissed?

This can help to spice things up a little and drown out their idle chit-chat.

But do be careful not to put yourself into any danger.

Maybe pre-order a cab for midnight and aim to board it **ALONE**!

the boring date

So you've matched with a right sort, exchanged hours of exciting messages and you have the date of your life lined up at the end of the week... of course you stalked the family, practiced your new 'married' signature and chose the names for your children.

Then the unexpected happens...
WTF? Often you will know at first glance and feel instantly deflated...

What happened to all the clever banter and witty repartee?
What's going on with their hair?
I don't remember them mentioning they were a midget!?

Try your hardest to look interested whilst not getting caught checking the time too often, or blatantly joining into the next table's conversation.

39

One option is to try to entertain yourself by sharing made-up facts about you and your family!

"My Dad is best mates with Boris Johnson".

You could also demonstrate the different types of birdsong you've learned throughout those years
as a twitcher?

Do whatever you have to, but try to be courteous. Give them at least half an hour and finish your drink, before you get the hell out of there.

Make a swift, polite getaway and I would suggest blocking them to cause any more embarrassment for either of you.

Get back on tinder and arrange a rebound date ASAP.

41

double dating

Dates are a bit like buses, nothing for ages, then they all turn up at once.

Do not turn any dates down, if you have to (or if you feel like a bit of a challenge) feel free to schedule more than one date in an evening. Clearly you're in demand. You've got to give everyone a chance right?

You're hot property... so utilise your time.

Early drinks with number one and a late dinner with date number two.

Busy people are more attractive anyway. You'll be glad of this executive decision when date number one is boring you to tears and their breath is making your eyes water.

Plan your excuse and departure (a college reunion that's been planned for ages) ahead of time with number one and always stick to the original plan.

Just use your loaf when booking the second date venue.

the 3 date rule

Now we'd all love to feel 'thunderbolt city' the moment we lock eyes with someone, however some of us live in the real world (apparently) and this doesn't always happen.

Some good things take time.
If your date seems 'good on paper' but there are no fireworks at first, give them another chance.

There could be a host of reasons why they're not firing on all cylinders.
Maybe they got a nasty speeding ticket en-route to the date?
Sudden fatality in the family?
Trapped wind?

Persevere, but don't clutch at straws.
3 strikes and they're out.

Still no butterflies after 3 dates??
NEXTTTTT!!!!!!

After all, you can't flog a dead horse.

tinder @ the races

Heading for a day at the races?

The Grand National, Royal Ascot, or the cheap seats at Goodwood? It doesn't matter... grab every opportunity.

Fellow tinder users are likely to have loosened up after a few glasses of fizz and might be in the mood for a celebration.

There's nothing like those sharp suits, flamboyant headgear and the smell of cash to whet your appetite and ensure the going is firm.

Adjust that radius slider, study the form and hedge your bets.

Check out tinder!

tindering @ festivals

For all you hipsters this festival season.

Let's face it, Glastonbury alone is practically the size of most people's hometowns.

I'm not recommending this (without a supply of industrial strength baby wipes) but I'm never one to rule anything out.

If your phone is lucky enough to have an internet connection then why not adjust the radius slider and check out who's on the market.

Those long weekends could get chilly in a soggy tent all on your tod.

In for a penny in for a pound.

the text of death

Like someone but you don't want to rip their clothes off? No spark?

Don't muck about.

Be direct, diplomatic and complimentary.

Suggest to stay friends without the intention of doing so.

At this point remember that 9/10 people want to be more than just 'mates'.

Time to cut your losses.

Get back on tinder!

swiping @ Christmas

For those who weren't listening, tinder uses your phones GPS to find potential matches.

Great!! Until half the country relocates over the Christmas break.
This is a logistical dating nightmare.

For some people this may not be an issue.

However, if you find yourself feeling fruity after a few festive mulled wines and can't stomach another round of trivial pursuit in a very warm living room with the family, then crack on my friend as I'm sure you're not alone.

Looking for something slightly more serious? Maybe lay off the app for a fortnight or so, give your blower a rest, spend some quality time with your Nan, or self-administer yourself into a food and wine coma.

Either way, 'tis the season to be jolly, enjoy yourself, overindulge, don't lose those gift receipts, use protection, maybe carry a toothbrush.

59

bill etiquette

We've all been there, and some people overcomplicate this - don't.

Call me old-fashioned, but as a rule
I wouldn't expect a girl to buy
the first drink - so guys assume
you're paying.

Not for the whole evening of course,
but the first couple of drinks is a kind
gesture - go armed with cash.

Look at it as an investment, market
research, a piss up, whatever.

Remember there's no such thing
as a free lunch.

instagram

You may notice you have the option
to link your instagram account
to your profile.

This gives viewers and potential
matches an opportunity to delve
deeper into your private life and gives
an insight into your personality.

This can go one of two ways, you may
think WOW this person has potential,
we drink the same coffee and we eat
the same food.

But...

You may get more than you bargained for! Before you know it your 174 weeks deep into your potentials profile and your left wondering if they had a nice time in Dubai with their ex.

Personally I advise against including Instagram, in fact leave it well alone. Get to know someone before you judge them.

No I don't fancy a #cheekynandos.

it's only a game

Tinder candidly refers to itself as a 'game' giving you the option to 'keep playing' after each match.
Even though you're 'playing against real life contestants' try not to get caught up in it all.

Prepare yourself for some total weirdos and time-wasters.
You will inevitably have dozens of matches but realistically only communicate with a small percentage of these.

You may wind up exchanging several messages with someone who tickles your fancy, to later be given the cold shoulder. Do not be disheartened.

My personal thoughts in this situation were always 'you're on effing tinder mate - the game's up' but you never know, they might be busy working on the space station or finding the cure for cancer - good for them.

Now folks I've divulged as much as I care to (or can remember) and truly hope this is of use.

Not keen on my advice? Then feel free to re-gift and upcycle this mini dating manual.

Go tinder!! x

glossary

The 3 date rule - the understanding to discard a 'datee' after 3 dates if little spark and no fireworks.

Bio - a short description of one's self, stating relevant facts excluding convictions.

Block - a term used to protect you in social media to stop a specific person contacting you or seeing your profile 'to block someone' (also comes in handy when friends with your Manager at work and you call in sick to go to a festival).

Double Dating - to arrange multiple dates over 24hrs.

Good on paper - when potential 'datee' marital status, interests and salary seem appealing and you assume you're a perfect match 'they seem good on paper'.

GPS - Global Positioning System

GRINDR - a hook-up app (predominantly for penetration) aimed at promiscuous homosexuals.

Selfie - a narcissistic photograph taken by one's self, often includes half an arm and a stupid face.

Thunderbolt city - instant attraction to somebody, to feel fireworks going off, having that spark, to constantly wander around smiling gormlessley making no sense.

TMI - too much information

WTF - what the fuck?

Yamas - cheers (to anyone who hasn't been to Greece).